AF228907

WAYNE GRETZKY

VS.

ALEX OVECHKIN

HOCKEY LEGENDS FACE OFF

by Elliott Smith

CAPSTONE PRESS
a capstone imprint

Published by Capstone Press, an imprint of Capstone
1710 Roe Crest Drive, North Mankato, Minnesota 56003
capstonepub.com

Library of Congress Cataloging-in-Publication Data

Names: Smith, Elliott, 1976- author.
Title: Wayne Gretzky vs. Alex Ovechkin : hockey legends face off / by Elliott Smith. Other titles: Wayne Gretzky versus Alex Ovechkin
Description: North Mankato, : Capstone Press, 2025.
Series: Sports illustrated kids. Legend vs. legend | Includes bibliographical references and index.
Audience: Ages 9-11 | Audience: Grades 4-6
Summary: "Wayne Gretzky and Alex Ovechkin are hockey superstars! Between the two, Gretzky has the most career points, but Ovechkin has more game-winning goals. So which one is the all-time best? Young readers can decide for themselves by comparing the fantastic feats and stunning stats of two legendary pro hockey players"-- Provided by publisher.
Identifiers: LCCN 2024032147 (print) | LCCN 2024032148 (ebook) | ISBN 9781669089438 (hardcover) | ISBN 9781669089612 (paperback) | ISBN 9781669089476 (pdf) ISBN 9781669089629 (epub) | ISBN 9781669089636 (kindle edition)
Subjects: LCSH: Gretzky, Wayne, 1961---Juvenile literature. | Ovechkin, Alexander, 1985---Juvenile literature. | Hockey--Statistics--Juvenile literature.
Classification: LCC GV848.5.G73 S65 2025 (print) | LCC GV848.5.G73 (ebook) | DDC 796.962/092 [B]--dc23/eng/20240919
LC record available at https://lccn.loc.gov/2024032147
LC ebook record available at https://lccn.loc.gov/2024032148

Editorial Credits
Editor: Ericka Smith; Designer: Tracy Davies; Media Researcher: Svetlana Zhurkin; Production Specialist: Whitney Schaefer

Image Credits
Associated Press: Pugliese, 16, Ron Frehm, 19; Getty Images: Allsport/Al Bello, cover (left), Allsport/Joe Patronite, 28, Allsport/Rick Stewart, 15, Allsport/Todd Warshaw, 7, Bongarts/Mark Sandten, 24, Bruce Bennett, 8, 17, 23, 25, 27, Claus Andersen, 22, Glenn Cratty, 21, Mike Powell, 12, Mitchell Layton, 9, Patrick Smith, cover (right), 13, 14, 18, 29, Richard Wolowicz, 20, Rick Stewart, 10, Rob Carr, 11; Newscom: Cal Sport Media/John Crouch, 26; Shutterstock: saicle (background), cover and throughout; Sports Illustrated: Damian Strohmeyer, 6, Manny Millan, 4, Robert Beck, 5

Printed in the United States   6350

CONTENTS

** * * All stats are current through the 2023–24 NHL season. * * **
Words in **bold** appear in the glossary.

Hockey Legends Face Off!

Wayne Gretzky and Alexander (Alex) Ovechkin are two of the greatest hockey players of all time. They're superstars of the National Hockey League (NHL). Gretzky is called "the Great One." Ovechkin is nicknamed "the Great Eight." Gretzky is known for his speed. And Ovechkin has a powerful shot.

But which player is the best in the league? Let's find out!

Wayne Gretzky

Alex Ovechkin

THE MATCHUP	Born	City
Gretzky	Jan. 26, 1961	Brantford, Ontario, Canada
Ovechkin	Sept. 17, 1985	Moscow, Russia, USSR

Height and Weight

Ovechkin's and Gretzky's success proves there's no right body type for hockey. Ovechkin has a **burly** frame. But he has great skating skills. Gretzky had a slight build. But he knew how to utilize every inch of his frame to gain an advantage!

Ovechkin playing in a 2012 game against the Boston Bruins

Gretzky playing for Canada in an Olympic game against Sweden

THE MATCHUP	Height	Weight
Ovechkin	6 feet, 3 inches (191 centimeters)	238 pounds (108 kilograms)
Gretzky	6 feet (183 cm)	185 pounds (84 kg)

Draft Day

Gretzky and Ovechkin were both famous as teenagers. Gretzky wasn't **drafted** by an NHL team. He made his **debut** in 1978 with the Indianapolis Racers. The Racers were part of the now **defunct** World Hockey League (WHL). Ovechkin was the first pick in the 2004 NHL draft.

Gretzky after signing with the Racers in 1978

Ovechkin showing off his jersey after being drafted by the Washington Capitals

THE MATCHUP	Year Signed/ Drafted	Age	Team
Gretzky	1978	17	Indianapolis Racers
Ovechkin	2004	18	Washington Capitals

Position

Both players stayed in the thick of the action. Gretzky was a center. He was in the middle of the ice, leading his team's offense. As a center, he could pass easily. Ovechkin is a left winger. He lines up alongside the center. He's always ready to receive a pass and shoot the puck.

Gretzky playing for the New York Rangers in 1996

Ovechkin shooting in a 2021 game

THE MATCHUP	Position
Gretzky	Center
Ovechkin	Left Wing

Games Played

Gretzky and Ovechkin have had long, successful careers. Gretzky played for 21 seasons. Ovechkin is still going strong. He finished his 19th season in 2024.

Gretzky playing during his 11th season

Ovechkin playing during his 19th season with the Washington Capitals

THE MATCHUP	Seasons Played	Games Played	Team(s)
Gretzky	21	1,487	Indianapolis Racers, Edmonton Oilers, Los Angeles Kings, St. Louis Blues, New York Rangers
Ovechkin	19	1,426	Washington Capitals

Best Skill

Ovechkin's slap shot makes him dangerous from anywhere on the ice. But he likes to take shots from just right of the goaltender. He can send a puck toward the goal at about 100 miles per hour (161 kilometers per hour).

Gretzky's **agility** helped him skate fast and weave through defenders. He never lost his balance!

Ovechkin taking a shot during a 2022 game

Gretzky moving the puck across the ice during a 1990 game against the Minnesota North Stars

THE MATCHUP	Best Skill
Ovechkin	Shooting
Gretzky	Skating

Goal Scoring

Gretzky and Ovechkin are the top two goal scorers in NHL history. Over his career, Gretzky scored 894 goals. He scored a record 92 goals during the 1981–82 season. Ovechkin hopes to beat Gretzky. He ended the 2023–24 season with 853 goals. He has 129 game-winning goals.

Gretzky scoring his 800th goal

Ovechkin celebrating his goal against the Philadelphia Flyers in 2024

THE MATCHUP	Career Goals	Season High	Game-Winning Goals
Gretzky	894	92	91
Ovechkin	853	65	129

Assists

Ovechkin and Gretzky aren't just great scorers. They're skilled passers too. Ovechkin has 697 **assists**. Gretzky made 1,963 assists—the most in NHL history.

Ovechkin making a pass during a 2019 game

Gretzky celebrating after passing the puck to his teammate for a game-winnning goal

THE MATCHUP	Assists
Ovechkin	697
Gretzky	1,963

All-Star Appearances

The best of the best play in the All-Star Game. Both Ovechkin and Gretzky have had memorable moments during the **contest**. Ovechkin has played in eight All-Star Games. He's scored eight times. Gretzky played in 18 All-Star Games. He made 13 goals. That's the most in NHL history.

Ovechkin taking a shot in the 2009 NHL All-Star Game

Gretzky competing in the 1997 NHL All-Star Game

THE MATCHUP	All-Star Appearances	All-Star Goals
Ovechkin	8	8
Gretzky	18	13

Season Honors

Both Ovechkin and Gretzky have earned high honors. Ovechkin has won the Most Valuable Player (MVP) award three times. He's also captured the trophy for most goals in a season nine times. Gretzky was named MVP nine times and won the league's **sportsmanship** trophy five times. He's also been the top goal scorer in the league five times.

Ovechkin with the Maurice Richard Trophy (far left) and the Hart Memorial Trophy (second from right)

Gretzky with the Hart Memorial Trophy in 1989

THE MATCHUP	MVP Awards Hart Memorial Trophy, Starting in 1924	Most Goals in a Season Awards Maurice Richard Trophy, Starting in 1998	Sportsmanship Awards Lady Byng Memorial Trophy, Starting in 1925
Ovechkin	3	9	0
Gretzky	9	5	5

Olympic Glory

Hockey is a popular Olympic sport. Gretzky played in the 1998 Olympics for Canada. But the team finished in fourth place. He did win a gold medal as the **executive director** of Canada's team in 2002. Ovechkin has played in the Olympics three times for Russia. But he has yet to win a gold medal.

Gretzky playing for Canada in the 1998 Olympics

Ovechkin playing for Team Russia during the 2014 Winter Olympics

THE MATCHUP	Olympic Appearances
Gretzky	1
Ovechkin	3

Championship Wins

Skating with the Stanley Cup is a special moment for NHL players. After 13 seasons in the league, Ovechkin finally won a **championship** in 2018. And Gretzky was part of the Edmonton Oilers **dynasty** in the 1980s. They won four Stanley Cups.

Ovechkin celebrating the Capitals' Stanley Cup win in 2018

Gretzky celebrating a 1986 Stanley Cup win with the Edmonton Oilers

THE MATCHUP	Stanley Cup Wins
Ovechkin	1
Gretzky	4

Who Is the Best?

Alex Ovechkin and Wayne Gretzky are legendary hockey players. Gretzky has the lead in goals (for now). He also has more assists. But Ovechkin has a more powerful shot and more game-winning goals. He also has the legacy of playing for one team and reshaping its history.

Who is the best? You make the call!

Gretzky playing for the St. Louis Blues in 1996

Ovechkin in a 2023 game against the New York Rangers

Glossary

agility (uh-JIH-luh-tee)—the ability to move fast and easily

assist (uh-SIST)—a pass that leads to a goal

burly (BUHR-lee)—strongly and heavily built

championship (CHAM-pee-uhn-ship)—a final match that determines who will be the overall winner

contest (KAHN-test)—a game or competition

debut (DAY-byoo)—an athlete's first competition

defunct (dih-FUHNKT)—no longer in existence

draft (DRAFT)—to select a player to play on one's team

dynasty (DYE-nuh-stee)—a team that wins multiple championships over a period of several years

executive director (ig-ZE-kyuh-tiv duh-REK-tuhr)—the decision-maker for an Olympic hockey team

sportsmanship (SPORTS-muhn-ship)—fair and respectful behavior when playing a sport

Read More

Berglund, Bruce. *Hockey Records Smashed!*
North Mankato, MN: Capstone, 2024.

Leed, Percy. *Pro Hockey by the Numbers*.
Minneapolis: Lerner, 2024.

Walker, Tracy Sue. *Wayne Gretzky: The Great One*.
Minneapolis: Lerner, 2023.

Internet Sites

Gretzky: Biography
gretzky.com/bio.php

Kiddle: National Hockey League Facts for Kids
kids.kiddle.co/National_Hockey_League

Sports Illustrated Kids: Catching Up with Alex Ovechkin
sikids.com/kid-reporter/catching-alex-ovechkin

Index

About the Author

Elliott Smith is a freelance writer, editor, and author. He has covered a wide variety of subjects—including sports, entertainment, and travel—for newspapers, magazines, and websites. He has written more than 70 children's books, both fiction and nonfiction. He lives in the Washington, DC, area with his wife and two children.